TOMMY

FIRST WORLD WAR SOLDIER

CHRIS MCNAB

On 4 August 1914, Britain entered a war like no other in its history.
On the Western Front alone, winding its muddy track down through
Belgium and France, this conflict would draw in 4 million British and
British Empire soldiers, the vast majority of whom were volunteers in the
'New Armies' or straightforward conscripts, given frequently questionable
training and then sent to war in mainland Europe. A total of 1.7 million
of them would either lose their lives or suffer debilitating wounds.

'Tommy Atkins', a convenient label for the typical British Army
infantryman of this period, has become an enduring figure of modern
British history. His precise conceptual origins are uncertain. References to
him first appear in soldiers' letters of the 18th century, but a more official
acknowledgement came in 1815, when Private Thomas Atkins of
No. 6 Troop, 6th Dragoons, was used as an example of how to fill
out identity information in the *Soldier's Pocket Book*. With his name
thereafter in wide distribution, 'Tommy' had become a standard
shorthand for the British soldier by the beginning of the 20th century.

This book explores the reality of the Tommy's life on the Western Front
between 1914 and 1918. The figure of the Tommy has been highly
mythologized. War poets and many historians have surrounded him with
pathos and poppies, a terrible aura of lost innocence and futile courage.
The experience of the Tommy could be tragic and horrifying, of that there
can be no doubt. Yet alongside the horror of war, the full story of Tommy
Atkins has greater depths than is often appreciated.

*Front Cover: The face of despondancy: a British prisoner of war, captured during the German
offensives of 1918. Unknown to him, the war had only months left to run.*

B ritain's opening shots in the First World War on the Western Front were fired by the forces of its regular army, just 233,000 men strong at the time. The British Expeditionary Force (BEF) component deployed into France and Belgium in August 1914 initially consisted of six infantry divisions and one cavalry division, some 150,000 soldiers. Germany, by contrast, could draw on a standing army of about 900,000 men; add all types of reservist and its military strength climbed to 3.5 million. The French Army had 700,000 men on its peacetime establishment. Even including the resources of Britain's part-time Territorial Force – 272,000 men in 1914 – and its 64,000-strong Special Reserve, Britain was not prepared for the long war of attrition that the Western Front became. It quickly became clear to the British government that it would have to draw on wider resources of manpower.

▼ *Lord Haldane (right), the great army reformer, and Sir John French, the Inspector-General of the Army, observe troop manoeuvres around Aldershot, c. 1912.*

NEW ARMIES

Although frequently criticized in historical writings, the British Secretary of State for War, Field Marshal Horatio Kitchener, at least understood that the incipient war would evolve into a long-term struggle. Large volumes of trained soldiers were the key to sustaining the effort, and to this end Kitchener persuaded the government to sanction an army expansion to the tune of 500,000 men. A masterfully persuasive publicity campaign called for volunteers, and British men responded in their droves. The 500,000-man limit was soon smashed by both public enthusiasm and grim military necessity – and 2,466,719 volunteers had enlisted by the end of 1915 into what were known as 'Kitchener's Armies' or the 'New Armies'.

Yet the initial surge of enlistment naturally subsided to concerning levels. In early 1916, therefore, as the war continued to swallow manpower, voluntary enlistment ceased and the Military Service Act 1916 – compulsory conscription – was introduced. Conscription

THE ACCRINGTON PALS

The 11th (Service) Battalion (Accrington) East Lancashire Regiment, known as the 'Accrington Pals', was formed in September 1914 as men from the Accrington area (plus the nearby towns of Burnley, Chorley and Blackburn) flocked to Kitchener's New Armies. Officers were nominated by Accrington's mayor. The battalion reached full strength – 1,100 men – in just two weeks, and on 1 July 1916 some 720 of the 'Pals' participated in an attack on Serre on the first day of the Somme campaign. By the end of the day, 584 were dead, wounded or missing, casualty figures that ripped the heart from the Lancashire communities back home.

▲ *A group of Accrington Pals wait for a haircut or shave from fellow 'Pal' and barber William Henry Bentley. The photo is thought to have been taken at Penkridge Bank Camp, Staffordshire, in 1915.*

▲ *An artwork showing the charge of the 5th Lancers at Elandslaagte during the Second Boer War in October 1899. When the British Army entered the First World War, its recent experience was largely in colonial conflicts.*

was not necessarily the magic ticket that might be supposed – all eligible males between 19 and 41 became available for service, but hundreds of thousands were excluded on various exemption criteria, such as being in essential war work or having medical problems. Recruitment actually declined annually, from 1.2 million in 1916 to 800,000 in 1917, as Britain scraped the bottom of the barrel in its hunt for fresh recruits.

UNITS AND FORMATIONS

The British Army was formed, in ascending order of scale, in sections, platoons, companies, battalions, regiments, brigades, divisions, corps and armies. The soldier's core unit was his battalion, which might stay under the auspices of one division, or be moved between divisions. (As a guide to scale, in 1916 a brigade typically had four battalions, and a division had three brigades.) A battalion theoretically numbered about 1,000 men, but the attrition of war and other factors could reduce its practical strength to a few hundred.

The volunteerism of the New Armies meant that battalions often had a very regional identity, as entire local groups of young men, such as factory workers or members of sports clubs, joined up together. Although many regionally titled battalions had large components of non-native personnel, a situation that became more pronounced as the war went on, the fact remained that a battalion devastated in action often meant a community equally devastated back in Britain.

JOINING UP

From today's less patriotic times, it is hard to picture the enthusiasm (and the social pressure) for joining the armed services in 1914. Vast queues snaked out of recruitment offices around the country. On one day alone – 3 September 1914 – 33,204 men joined up. The British Army was flooded with fresh manpower almost immediately, all of them eager not to 'miss the show'.

TEETHING TROUBLES

The explosive expansion of the British Army (five new armies, a total of 30 divisions, were established in September alone) brought problems of its own. Although hundreds of thousands successfully joined up, many others were left frustrated when battalions reached full strength, or they failed the Army's medical. Large numbers of inexperienced medical personnel were recruited to expedite the process and, encouraged by a 2s 6d (approximately £5 in today's money) fee for every man examined, they could churn through candidates with little medical rigour. First-hand accounts from veterans also noted that dozens of men were simply taken off to

YOUR COUNTRY'S CALL

Isn't this worth fighting for?

ENLIST NOW

▲ A poster produced by the Parliamentary Recruiting Committee in 1915, playing on the love of country to encourage men to enlist in the British Army.

◀ Crowds of young men gather outside the Central London Recruiting Depot in 1914, eager to join the armed forces and go off to war.

basic training without seeing a doctor at all. Age was another barrier to military service, but it wasn't fail-safe. The minimum age of service was 19, but tens of thousands of younger men circumvented the stipulation fraudulently. (Men could join the regular army at age 18, but were not eligible for foreign service until they turned 19.) One young soldier of the 2nd Battalion, 6th Cheshire Regiment (2/6th Cheshire Regiment) had not even cleared the age of 14 when he joined up in November 1914. The minimum age for foreign service was reduced to 18 in April 1918, in response to the Germans' spring offensives.

▶ *New recruits to the London Scottish Regiment in 1914 have the chance to practise basic rifle drill, despite the fact that they have not yet received uniforms.*

CONSCIENTIOUS OBJECTORS

With the implementation of the Military Service Act 1916, British recruiters encountered some 16,000 conscientious objectors, men who for ethical or religious beliefs refused to join the armed forces, or at least serve as combatants. They had to justify themselves before a Military Service Tribunal, who compelled significant numbers to perform non-combatant duties within the armed services, such as working as stretcher-bearers, or diverted them to essential industries like farming. Many also ended up in prison for their beliefs, where they tended to be treated with brutality and disdain.

▲ *Two conscientious objectors, handcuffed to one another, are led away from a police station in 1916. Despite their ethical stance, they could still end up at the front in non-combat roles.*

IN SERVICE

Another issue raised by the rapid creation of the New Armies was that of training. Most regular army soldiers had received pre-war instruction under experienced officers and non-commissioned officers (NCOs), and with predictable kit and weaponry. Many New Armies recruits, by contrast, frequently found themselves in cold, damp tent camps without weapons or proper uniforms, or simply billeted in local pubs or other accommodation. (One soldier remembered sleeping on a pub billiard table for several nights.) Gunner Bill Sugden, when arriving at a camp in Newhaven, East Sussex, noted that 'Everything is rough. The camp is like a quagmire, and no floorboards in the tent ... Had a shave with difficulty and cold water. Truly last night I wished I was dead.' Training the newly expanded army was also troubled by a lack of experienced officers, and all manner of reservist and retired officers were pressed into service.

After roughly two months of basic training was completed in Britain, dominated by PT (known then as 'Swedish Drill'), marksmanship, bayonet drill and field craft, the Tommy and his comrades were shipped out overseas. In time, professionalism and more manageable numbers of recruits took hold. The fact remains, however, that many soldiers went to the battlefields of France or Belgium woefully under-prepared to fight.

Types of Tommy

The British Army was a vast organization, and its soldiers performed a huge variety of different roles. Following basic training, a recruit would go on to receive specialist instruction within the context of his branch of service – signaller, medic, machine gunner, artilleryman, etc. This training would continue when posted overseas, both before going to the front and in the rear areas when a soldier was out of the line.

Non-Combatants

A critical, though far from watertight, distinction amongst British Army soldiers was that between combatants and non-combatants. One important point to note is that while in subsequent conflicts non-combatant support soldiers significantly outnumbered actual fighting men, in the First World War the reverse was true. Front-line infantry were actually around double the strength of the rear-echelon men.

The British Army relied on numerous support formations to keep the military machine in motion at the front. A soldier in the Army Service Corps (ASC), for example, was one amongst c. 400,000 personnel responsible for logistics.

He might find himself in a workshop or warehouse in a major Base Depot established around a Channel port, or he might belong to a Horse Transport Company or Mechanical Transport Company, making perilous journeys to the front under German shellfire to deliver supplies or shift wounded soldiers to the rear.

▲ A British artilleryman stands amidst a heavy artillery ammunition dump. Personalized messages, such as 'A present for Jerry' seen here, were frequently scrawled on shells.

◄ A British machine-gun team conduct training with a Maxim machine gun in England, c. 1915. The white cap bands indicate that these men are officer cadets.

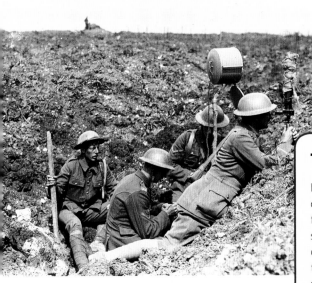

The men of the Army Ordnance Corps (AOC), by contrast, dealt with the supply, storage and maintenance of munitions. Various labour/pioneer units (an entire Labour Corps was formed in 1917) performed an inexhaustible range of manual tasks, both behind the front lines and within the trenches. 'Rear-echelon' was often an unfair label for such men, who were frequently in harm's way.

FIGHTING MEN

While there was diversity in the support services, the same was also true of combatants. Royal Artillery gunners could find themselves either manning a stumpy trench mortar in a mud-filled trench, or positioned behind a heavy howitzer some miles behind the front line. Royal Engineers not only delivered numerous rear-area engineering duties, but also performed reconnaissance (via the Field Survey units), conducted poison gas attacks (Special Companies) and undertook grim mining operations (Tunnelling Companies – see panel). Men of the Signals Companies had the thankless job of laying field telephone cables across shell-ploughed battlefields.

TUNNELLING COMPANIES

In February 1915, the Royal Engineers began forming eight Tunnelling Companies, utilizing men drawn from the ranks, but also recruiting civilian mining specialists. Their principal role, and that of the 13 other such companies subsequently formed, was to dig tunnels covertly under the enemy trenches and emplace explosives, to be detonated at the beginning of an offensive, although they were also used for counter-mining operations against German tunnellers. The work was perilous, dark and dirty. On several occasions British tunnellers accidentally met German equivalents underground, resulting in subterranean close-quarters fighting. There were also the constant dangers of tunnel collapse and of handling explosives in confined spaces. A little extra pay was given for such nerve-wracking duties.

▲ British tunnellers dig one of 21 mine shafts under the Messines Ridge in 1917. Some 19 of the mines were filled with explosives and detonated under German positions on 7 June 1917.

OFFICERS AND MEN

E ven amongst the humble infantry units at the front, there were specialisms. Infantry sections of about 12 men, for example, were subdivided into 'bombers' and 'bayonet men', the former clearing enemy trenches with grenades, the latter securing each cleared trench section. In support, soldiers of the Machine Gun Corps poured automatic fire onto the enemy positions.

The British Army was, like any large human machine, apt to periodic breakdowns and malfunctions. Yet on the whole it kept working reasonably efficiently for four years of devastating war. The British infantryman's immediate world was his section, theoretically 12 men strong and led by an NCO – a corporal or a sergeant. The NCOs were the true backbone of the army, and had to perform a multitude of roles ranging from counsellor and administrator through to section assault leader. W. Walker, a soldier in the 13th Northumberland Fusiliers, remembers how just before an attack at the battle of Loos in September 1915 'There was no officer near us, so an aged sergeant, who ought to have been at home with his wife, took charge of us.' The sergeant was later seen urging the men across the battlefield into a storm of fire, shouting 'Come on, lads, we've got to do it.' And yet the rush to recruit in 1914 and 1915 meant that many men were promoted to NCO rank without the commensurate experience. In his book *Tommy*, military historian Richard Holmes notes that many men 'were promoted before they even had uniforms to sew their stripes to'. Experienced regular army NCOs, therefore, would provide invaluable advice to the men under them, although such NCOs were often in short supply.

▲ *Sir John French (second from left), commander-in-chief of the British Expeditionary Force, with his aides-de-camp at headquarters in France.*

◀ *NCOs could be the object of humour as well as affection, as seen in this cartoon from a soldier's autograph book.*

LEADERS OF MEN

Above the section, the two most meaningful units for the infantryman were the platoon and the company. The platoon consisted of four sections, and was led by a lieutenant or second lieutenant, while the company was composed of four platoons led by a major or captain. (Total theoretical strength of a company was 227 men, including the company headquarters staff.) In turn, four companies made up the battalion, typically led by a lieutenant colonel. The officers, just as with the privates and NCOs, varied tremendously in quality and background. The demand for officers in 1914 far outstretched supply, meaning that many individuals were

◀ *British soldiers begin an assault with fixed bayonets. Good NCOs were critical during such attacks, keeping the men together as a coherent group and maintaining focus on the objective.*

▼ *Even trench life could have its refinements. Here a group of officers from the 12th Battalion, East Yorkshire Regiment, take time to wash and shave in their well-maintained dugout near Rolincourt, January 1918.*

rapidly over-promoted, or that former officers, many with experience only of far-flung colonial outposts, were drawn back into service. In some cases, newly formed regional battalions had officers simply appointed from the citizenry by the local mayor or other dignitary.

While the nobility was still very much represented amongst the officer class, during the First World War the middle classes came to occupy a broad swathe of the officer posts. Actual wartime commissions and promotions, however, were generally temporary, the officer receiving a temporary rank related to a specific command, and reverting to his normal regimental rank once that command ceased or the conflict ended.

FRONTLINE COMMANDERS

The First World War was a uniquely dangerous conflict for officers, even for those of particularly high rank. An astonishing total of 58 British Army generals were killed during the war, and more divisional commanders (three) were killed at the battle of Loos than in the whole of the Second World War. Amongst the NCO and junior officer ranks, the sacrifice was appalling. A front-line subaltern serving on the Western Front in 1916–17 had a life expectancy of about six weeks. Suffering alongside their men, the officers often created profound bonds of loyalty with them.

OFFICERS' BRAVERY

The war diary entries of the 1st King's (Liverpool) Regiment in 1916 regularly chart the heroism of junior officers, including the following entry:

20th January: On this date our headquarters were heavily shelled, and a shell hit a house near our Battalion Headquarters and it was reported that two men were badly wounded. Captain Kerr RAMC and a Lieutenant Towers dashed across the road to give them assistance. As they were clearing away bricks and rubbish which had fallen on the men, another shell landed in the same place and Lieutenant Towers was mortally wounded and died on his way to Béthune.

TRENCHES – CREATING A FRONT LINE

The Western Front was defined by static trench warfare, once the advances and retreats of 1914 had come to a standstill. As a general rule, trench systems consisted of fire trenches and communication trenches. The former were the fighting positions, set roughly parallel to one another and overlooking the enemy defences, depending on the dictates of terrain. A typical arrangement would consist of a front line (the foremost trench, also known as the 'main fire trench') plus a support line and then a reserve line further back. These lines would be connected by communication trenches, and sometimes 'sap' trenches stretched out beyond the main fire trench as advance listening posts in 'no-man's-land' – the open terrain between opposing trench lines.

STRUCTURE AND LAYOUT

While some trenches, particularly those dug and occupied temporarily during an offensive, could be hastily scraped-out affairs only a few feet deep, many were major works of engineering. Trenches were typically dug to a depth of 6–8ft (1.8–2.4m), depending on factors such as the water table and nature of the soil. On the Ypres salient, for example, the water table was just beneath the surface, so the trenches there were largely built up above ground using sandbags and earth deposits.

Once the crude trench was dug, its sides and parapets were revetted with timber and sandbags, while the floor consisted of duckboards, set above the earth to provide clearance (not always successfully) for drainage. Fire trenches also featured a 'firestep', a platform built roughly 2ft (0.6m) up the sides of the trench to enable the occupants to step up and (carefully) put their heads above the parapet (although it served a multitude of other functions – see panel). Support trenches incorporated dugouts cut deeper into the earth, serving as everything from accommodation to command posts. Dugouts ranged from being a crude earth chamber housing three or four men to a major underground structure capable of holding an entire company staff. Some extravagant examples (for the officers, naturally) were like strangely opulent homes, containing four-poster beds and large dining tables.

FIGHTING TRENCHES

Trenches were not linear affairs. They were dug in sections called 'bays' and 'traverses', demarcated by angled intersections – the design meant that the small-arms fire of an enemy soldier who had entered the trench, or the explosion of a shell, would affect only the men in that section, rather than all those in the trench line. Trench networks often developed into sprawling, labyrinthine affairs, necessitating

TOMMY'S FIRESTEP

'The firestep was the front-fighter's couch, bed-board, card table, workman's bench, universal shelf, only raised surface on which to set a thing down above the water level. He stood on it by night to watch the enemy; he sat upon it by day to watch him in a periscope. The nature, height and repair of firesteps was of great importance to the front-line soldier, especially before adequate dugouts became customary in all trenches.'
PRIVATE DAVID JONES, 15/ROYAL WELCH FUSILIERS

◀ A typical front-line trench. A sandbag shelter has been built against the wall of the trench; note also the duckboards on the floor to keep soldiers' feet out of the mud.

▶ A British wiring party rolling coils of barbed wire through the mud towards the front line in France, 1917. Installing barbed wire was generally performed at night, when there was less chance of the enemy spotting the group.

complicated signposts at key 'junctions' to prevent bewildered soldiers becoming hopelessly lost. No-man's-land had its own defences, principally in the form of thick barbed-wire belts laid in front of the trenches at night. These belts sometimes grew to tens of yards deep, and their purpose was to slow, rather than stop, an attack – an enemy trying to cut his way through would be prey to rifle, machine-gun and artillery fire.

When they functioned smoothly, trenches were impressive human systems. Yet for those who spent prolonged periods in them, the experience was rather different.

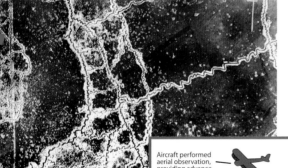

▲ An aerial photograph, taken in July 1917, shows the complexity of the British trench system between Loos and Hulluch, plus the multiple craters caused by shell explosions.

▶ Diagram detailing the trench system.

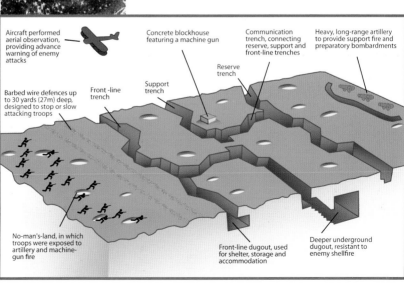

Aircraft performed aerial observation, providing advance warning of enemy attacks

Concrete blockhouse featuring a machine gun

Communication trench, connecting reserve, support and front-line trenches

Heavy, long-range artillery to provide support fire and preparatory bombardments

Reserve trench

Barbed wire defences up to 30 yards (27m) deep, designed to stop or slow attacking troops

Front-line trench

Support trench

No-man's-land, in which troops were exposed to artillery and machine-gun fire

Front-line dugout, used for shelter, storage and accommodation

Deeper underground dugout, resistant to enemy shellfire

Life in the Trenches

A new arrival on the front usually had a couple of days of settling in and instruction before he found himself manning a section of trench. This first posting was a dangerous time. He had to learn quickly the need to keep his head below the parapet at all times – enemy snipers often kept their rifles sighted and ready on dips in the parapet, hence the British put up cautionary signs reminding a soldier to duck through perilous sections. The soldier also had to distinguish between outgoing and incoming artillery, and be able to respond quickly to the latter. Trenches were remarkably good at protecting soldiers from anything other than a direct hit, although near strikes could destroy dugouts or bury a soldier under a collapsing trench wall.

Sanitation

As much as the soldier fought the enemy, he fought the environment. Heavy and prolonged rain could turn a trench into a mud pit. One soldier on the Somme recalled that 'the water from two hillsides has come into the valley and filled our trench in some places waist deep. In order to keep the trench from being absolutely waterlogged we have to pump continuously with the four pumps with which we have been supplied'. Constant wet conditions produced infectious skin complaints, including the flesh-rotting trench foot, which could induce gangrene in severe cases. During winter months, snow, ice and sub-zero temperatures led to hundreds of incidents of frostbite and hypothermia. And regardless of the season, lice and rats dogged the soldiers' trenches, clothing and morale. Trench rats grew particularly large and confident, feeding on corpses as well as scraps of food, and killing them grew into a minor industry for some soldiers. Lice were a more personal challenge,

▲ *Periscopes were essential equipment for looking over a trench parapet, keeping the viewer safe out of sight of enemy snipers across no-man's-land.*

◄ *Complex trench systems required signposts to prevent soldiers getting lost within them. Here a young British soldier paints up some signpost boards, with homely sounding 'street' names that include 'Devil's Dyke', 'Happy Alley' and 'Love Lane'.*

▲ *Soldiers on active service were meant to receive about 4,000 calories every day. Mobile kitchens were provided to take hot food to the troops on the front line – but these soldiers have scrounged their own 'mobile kitchen' and are cooking on a stove in a trench at Ovillers, July 1916.*

living on skin and in clothing, and making life for the affected soldier horribly itchy. Bodily functions became logistical challenges in the trenches. Latrines consisted of little more than a deep hole with a board 'seat'. They became noisome places, frequently targeted by enemy artillery and, courtesy of clouds of persistent flies moving between latrines and food, they produced a variety of gastrointestinal illnesses.

ROUTINE

The daily routine for soldiers in the trenches usually began with a period of 'stand to' as dawn approached and broke, the men being ready in case of an enemy attack. This period lasted roughly 1½ hours, after which the men 'stood down' and ate breakfast. The rest of the day would be divided into weapons inspections, sentry duties and various labour tasks. There was another 'stand to' period around dusk, after which some soldiers would rotate through the night on sentry duty, usually trying to fight sleep after an exhausting and potentially lethal day.

TRENCH FOOD

Cuisine in the trenches was rudimentary at best. Staples included corned beef ('bully beef'), a meat and vegetable product called Maconochie, rissoles, 'hard tack' biscuits, bacon and sausages (particularly at breakfast), tinned pork fat and beans, bread, jam (especially Tickler's 'Plum and Apple') and cheese. Monotony was often the order of the day, broken only by food parcels from home, although these were generally issued by the battalion once the troops were out of the line. Hot food might be transported up communications trenches from cookers to the rear, but soldiers would also perform their own cooking on wood fires, improvised braziers, or the small solid-fuel 'Tommy cooker'. There were cases of groups of men suffering from asphyxiation from using such cookers in unventilated dugouts.

BEHIND THE LINES

An abiding popular myth about the British soldier of the First World War was that he spent months on end in the front-line trenches. This did occur during the first winter of the war, when front-line manpower was still deficient, but from 1915 a fairly strict regular rotation was implemented. At any one time, a division would have its battalions and companies deployed in either the front line, in reserve positions close behind the front, or at rest well behind the front. An individual Tommy might spend roughly four to eight days on the front line, then a similar period in support or reserve trenches further back (or in other rough-and-ready reserve accommodation), with regular trips to the rear.

CAMP CONDITIONS

Being pulled back from the front line into support or reserve positions by no means implied that a Tommy was free from danger. Enemy heavy artillery had considerable reach, so soldiers could still experience sudden, explosive death well behind the foremost trenches. Furthermore, units were still expected to work hard, such as

▲ British Army camps sometimes grew to huge proportions, and housed tens of thousands of men. This camp, consisting of tents and wooden huts, was located at Harfleur, France, and is here seen as it looked in March 1916.

by sending working parties to make trench repairs or help dig new positions.

Those who were truly pulled back from the lines found themselves in all manner of billets. Some went into tents or more substantial wooden huts in various camps. Others were billeted with local civilians, or found themselves sleeping in farmhouses or converted public buildings.

The camps in France and Belgium could be notably inhospitable. Camp discipline from military police and rear-area staff was frequently hard and nagging, and tents or huts could be inundated with the mud soldiers might have hoped to escape. As much as rest and recuperation, relief from the front often brought additional hard training and constant labour. Yet as one soldier remarked, 'Our rest camps in that beautiful wood at St Eloi seemed like paradise after hell ... We were usually tired by the end of the day, but it was good to climb into the tiers of beds,

◀ Life in the rear could take on a more relaxing pace than at the front. Here a group of fur-clad soldiers play cards in their tent camp c. 1915.

▲ Soldiers take a break in reserve trenches at Beaumont Hamel, France. In these positions the men could be called quickly back up to the front line if the enemy attacked.

with chicken-wire mattresses, and wonderful to be able to take off our heavy boots before we settled down to kip.'

LITTLE LUXURIES

Relief from the front not only provided the opportunity to clean up and get some (relative) rest, but it also presented some mental escapes for battle-worn troops. Pay built up while at the front could be indulged in local shops, bars, gambling establishments and, in time-honoured fashion, brothels. (The latter establishments featured red lights if aimed at regular soldiers, and blue lights for officers.) More salubrious entertainment, such as film showings or concerts, were provided by divisional concert parties, or by organizations such as the Young Men's Christian Association (YMCA). Regardless of the nature, such diversions were no doubt eagerly seized by men worn out by front-line tension.

ROTATIONS

This extract, from a war diary of the 13th Royal Sussex Regiment (3rd South Down), illustrates a typical pattern of rotation on the Western Front in June 1916:

1 June 1916: Relieved by 11th Sussex. A Company moved to Cambrin Point, B to Braddell Castle, C to Cuinchy Keep, Caters Post and Tourbieres.
5 June: Relieved 11th Sussex in same Cuinchy sector. A to right, D in centre, B on left. C in support in Esperanto Terrace. Patrols sent out, but fairly quiet.
8 June: Relieved by 11th Sussex, moved to billets in Annequin North.
10 June: Moved to Divisional Reserve at La Pannerie. Much attack practice undertaken.
16 June: Relieved 17th Lancashire Fusiliers in Ferme du Bois trenches. A Company on right, C in centre, D on left and B in support at Bute Street.

➤ A train pulls into London's Victoria Station and deposits soldiers on leave, eager to see families and friends. The signs on the platform advertise money-changing facilities for soldiers with little but French francs in their pockets.

KIT AND UNIFORM

The British Army's standard 1902 Pattern Service Dress uniform was a generally practical form of military dress. Its two primary elements were a khaki tunic and trousers, the former having four button-down patch pockets, brass buttons, an internal pocket under the tunic flap (which typically held a field dressing), shoulder straps featuring regimental insignia, and a turned-down collar. (Note that a cruder, less-expensive version of the tunic was produced from 1914, known as the 'Utility Tunic'.) The trousers were relatively close-fitting, and ran down into long cloth puttees wound from the top of the boot to just below the knee. Footwear came in the form of heavy, square-toed, reversed-hide B5 ammunition boots, with metal-studded soles.

EXTREME PROTECTION

At the beginning of the war, army headgear was a khaki cap with stiff brim and leather strap; the front of the cap displayed the regimental badge. By the end of 1914, this unyielding cap was replaced with a soft-brimmed, more utilitarian variety, known affectionately as the 'Gor Blimey' cap. Yet neither of these caps provided any protection against serious head injury, so in early 1916 the now-classic 'Helmet, Steel, Mk I' was introduced. Designed by John Leopold Brodie, it was a pressed-steel helmet with a wide brim, leather liner and chin strap, and weighed 1.3lb (0.59kg). The 'Brodie Helmet' gave decent protection against shrapnel and bullets, and undoubtedly saved lives at the front. Against the cold, an army greatcoat provided rather bulky warmth, but soldiers were also issued with

▲ New recruits were expected to maintain high standards of kit and appearance, at least until deployed to the front line. Here young officer cadets of the Cambridge University Officer Training Corps undergo kit inspection.

▼ A sergeant measures new recruits – still dressed in their civilian clothes though some are already wearing army caps – for their uniforms. A sewing machine is on hand to make any adjustments to the fit.

▲ *Portrait photographs were commonly taken of a recruit in his new uniform. Here 19-year-old Private Maurice E. Brewer of the 7th Battalion Border Regiment wears the typical tunic, trousers and cap issued to infantrymen during the war.*

GAS MASKS

From the spring of 1915, gas masks steadily became a standard feature of British Army kit on the Western Front. The first varieties were crude – sanitary pads or flannel pads soaked in supposedly gas-absorbing chemicals (including bicarbonate of soda and, *in extremis*, urine), strapped over the nose and mouth. Later in the year, 'smoke helmets' made an appearance. The 'helmet' was in fact a large chemically treated cloth hood, with eyepieces and a rubber mouth valve, which fitted over the entire head and neck. Then, in 1916, came the Small Box Respirator (SBR), a waterproof mask fitted with eyepieces and a tin cylinder filled with filtering chemicals, through which the wearer breathed. Wearing such masks was a horrible experience for prolonged periods, but it was preferable to the alternative.

sleeveless goatskin jerkins. The jerkins looked cosy, but actually served as little more than traps for rain, mud and lice. A rubberized rain cape functioned as both a groundsheet and an item of clothing, and were later known as 'Gas Capes' because of their ability to provide a small degree of protection from contamination by poison gas.

LOAD-CARRYING

Fully loaded, a British infantryman could head off to war carrying more than 80lb (36kg) of kit and weaponry. To do so, he utilized the 1908 Pattern webbing, a quite advanced load-carrying system for the time (equipment shortages meant that leather varieties were also in use). Made principally by the Mills Equipment Company, its basic frame was a wide web belt and two equally substantial braces. On these straps hung two ammunition pouches (each holding 75 rounds of 0.303in ammunition), a bayonet frog, entrenching tool handle attachment, entrenching tool head in a web cover, water bottle carrier, a small

haversack and large pack worn on the back. The haversack contained daily use items – shaving and washing kit, rations, cutlery and personal belongings – while the backpack typically held bulky items such as greatcoats and blankets. Neither the uniform nor the webbing were perfect, but they provided decent comfort and protection in the most arduous of settings.

▲ *Typical items in a soldier's mess kit, including a 'Tommy cooker' and fuel, enamelled mug, condensed milk, Maconochie army ration, army biscuits and Oxo cubes.*

The standard British Army rifle of the First World War was the 0.303in Short Magazine Lee-Enfield (SMLE). Despite a rough reception from numerous experts when it was first introduced into service in 1903, it carved out a near-legendary status in the 1914–18 war.

▲ *The Short Magazine Lee-Enfield (SMLE) Mk III was one of the finest rifles of the war, with a smooth bolt-action, a 10-round box magazine and a lethal range in excess of a mile.*

RIFLE AND BAYONET

The SMLE measured 44.57in (113.2cm) long, and featured wooden furniture that ran all the way to the muzzle, giving it a distinctive 'snub-nosed' appearance. It was fed from a 10-round box magazine, and the bolt-action was smooth and fast. Regular soldiers were trained to fire up to 15 rounds per minute; at the battle of Mons on 23 August 1914, German soldiers on the receiving end of BEF rifle fire thought that they were confronting machine guns. The 0.303in round was powerful. It could kill at over 1,000 yards (900m) and punch through 18in (45cm) of oak at 200 yards (180m). Given proper field maintenance, it was also superbly reliable, and its accuracy meant that by fitting appropriate sights the soldier could turn it into a sniper rifle. Allied to the SMLE was the 1907 Pattern Wilkinson Sword bayonet – 17in (43cm) of lethal steel. Yet, as post-war analysis showed, few actual bayonet casualties were inflicted. The bayonet's value was primarily for inducing psychological shock in the enemy, or for more utilitarian purposes in daily trench life, such as opening tins or killing rats.

MACHINE GUNS

The machine gun transformed infantry warfare. By 1914, a single belt-fed machine gun could generate the same firepower as about 20 riflemen firing at their maximum rate, and two or three machine guns deployed intelligently could devastate an entire batallion. For the British Army, the defining machine gun was the 0.303in Vickers, an improved variant of the original ground-breaking Maxim gun. A water-cooled gun mounted on a substantial tripod, the Vickers could send out devastating fire at 450 rounds per minute, hour after hour (in appropriate controlled bursts), creating a lethal 'beaten zone' out to ranges of 2,000 yards (1.8km). Importantly, it was ultra-reliable. In one famous incident, ten Vickers of the 100th Company, Machine Gun Corps, fired for 12 hours without a single breakdown, going through 100 barrels and a million rounds of ammunition in the process.

Vickers were initially thin on the ground – just two per infantry battalion – but the creation of the Machine Gun Corps in October 1915 saw their enhanced importance and distribution.

▲ *The British Pattern 1907 bayonet was a fearsome piece of steel, albeit one that carried more psychological effect than actual combat utility.*

◄ Two men wearing gas helmets operate a Vickers machine gun during the battle of the Somme in 1916. With its water-cooled barrel, the Vickers could fire belts of 0.303in ammunition at a rate of 450rpm, for prolonged periods.

▶ British soldiers in a trench clutch their SMLE rifles. Although the SMLE was shorter than many rifles, it could still be unwieldy in trench combat, a fact that drove the invention of the shorter, rapid-fire submachine gun.

Battalion firepower came increasingly from the lighter, bipod-mounted Lewis Gun, instantly recognizable with its 47-round flat pan magazine and voluminous cooling shroud around the barrel. The Lewis was more mobile on the attack than the heavy Vickers, so was an ideal assault weapon.

CLOSE QUARTERS

For trench clearance, the British Tommy relied on the stalwart 'pineapple' No. 5 fragmentation grenade designed by William Mills (who later established the Mills Munitions Factory in Birmingham), which entered service in 1915. At truly close quarters, however, common infantry would resort to a fearful array of improvised trench weapons, including combined knuckledusters and daggers, sharpened spades, and wooden posts stuck through with exposed nails. (Officers would rely on Webley service revolvers.) Using basic weapons against similarly armed opponents must have been an appalling experience, more reminiscent of the medieval era than the 20th century.

RIFLE VOLLEY

Corporal John Lucy describes here how British rifle fire stopped a German machine gun at the Aisne in 1914:

By lucky chance or instinct I saw the enemy machine gun. There it was, mounted daringly on the roof of a cottage, about six hundred yards away, and directly to my front. With all my strength I shrieked the range, described the target, and ordered five rounds rapid fire ... In about four seconds some thirty bullets were whistling about that dark spot near the chimney as we slammed in our rapid fire, glad to have some work to do, and gloriously, insanely and incredibly the German machine gun stopped firing.

Artillery was the drumbeat of the First World War. Even when the front was relatively quiet, artillery fire was commonly exchanged, sporadically snatching away lives through blast and shrapnel. As preparation for a major offensive, however, artillery barrages shook the heavens. In the week before the launch of the Somme offensive on 1 July 1916, some 1,500 artillery pieces hurled 1.7 million shrapnel and high-explosive shells into the German lines. The ubiquity of artillery, and its explosive force and long-range reach, meant that it accounted for some 60–70 per cent of all casualties in the war.

BRITISH ARTILLERY

British artillery was essentially divided into three branches. The Royal Horse Artillery (RHA) and Royal Field Artillery (RFA) were the front-line guns, deploying light- and medium-calibre pieces in support of the cavalry and infantry. The classic gun of the RFA was the Ordnance QF 13-pounder, while the backbone of the RFA was the Ordnance QF 18-pounder. Although such guns had ranges measured in thousands of yards, on many occasions a crew might emplace its gun well within enemy machine-gun and rifle

▲ *A lithograph depicting Royal Artillery field gunners firing point-blank into masses of enemy infantry advancing during the German offensives of 1918. Note the loader at the rear waiting to feed another shell into the breech.*

range, and there was always the threat of German counter-battery fire. One gunner, fighting at Le Cateau in August 1914, remembered how the 'gun shields were a mass of silver where they were riddled with bullets, and several guns received direct hits'.

The Royal Garrison Artillery manned the heavy long-range howitzers, and were positioned a good distance behind the front line. Its personnel used guns such as the BL 9.2in Howitzer, which, in its Mk II version, could fire a 290lb (130kg) high-explosive shell to a range in excess of 13,000 yards (12km). As their guns were only fired indirectly (i.e. at targets beyond visual range), their crews relied entirely on fire control from forward observers (including airborne observers), who communicated via either wired or, later, wireless means.

Beyond the firepower of the Royal Artillery, the infantry themselves had a range of minor fire-support weapons. These included several varieties of mortar ranging from 2in (5cm) spigot mortars

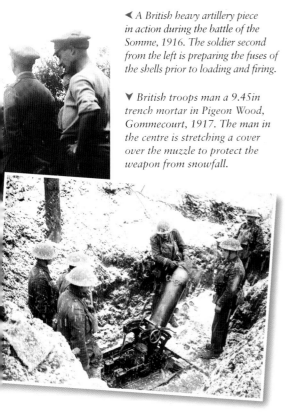

◄ *A British heavy artillery piece in action during the battle of the Somme, 1916. The soldier second from the left is preparing the fuses of the shells prior to loading and firing.*

▼ *British troops man a 9.45in trench mortar in Pigeon Wood, Gommecourt, 1917. The man in the centre is stretching a cover over the muzzle to protect the weapon from snowfall.*

to trench mortars of nearly 10in (25cm) calibre. The 3in and 4in (7.5cm and 10cm) mortars designed by Wilfred Stokes of the Ministry of Munitions became true ground-breakers, enabling an infantry company to provide decent fire support at a local level.

ENDURANCE

The British soldier in the trenches was, of course, a recipient of artillery fire as well as a beneficiary. Artillery shells had truly appalling physical effects, ripping apart entire sections of men in a single breath. One British soldier, fighting at Ginchy in August 1916, remembered seeing a German shell strike a group of men and witnessing 'a most tremendous burst of clay and earth go shooting up in the air – yes, even parts of human bodies – and then when the smoke cleared there was nothing left.' Often men would be buried alive by the earth thrown up from the explosion. Artillery was, for the Tommy, both his greatest friend and greatest enemy.

HORSE-DRAWN LOGISTICS

Although steam- and diesel-powered artillery tractors were used to pull artillery and supplies in the First World War (the Army Service Corps operated 22,000 trucks in France by January 1918), horses performed the bulk of artillery transportation. Indeed, every aspect of British Army logistics depended on literal horse power. As the war expanded, millions of horses were requisitioned or given voluntarily to service, the mounts as diverse as farm ponies and thoroughbred racehorses. The use of horses was a logistical challenge in itself, requiring hundreds of tons of fodder every day and extensive veterinary support services. They died in their hundreds of thousands, the hapless victims of shellfire, gas, bullets, neglect, overwork and exposure to harsh weather.

▲ *Horses and mules suffered terribly while working in the mud of the Western Front. Here two British soldiers attempt to free a mule stuck fast in the quagmire at Ypres, Belgium, in 1917.*

DISCIPLINE AND PUNISHMENT

The British Army of the First World War brought together millions of disparate men, of all ethical standards, into a common uniform. At the same time, the requisite expansion of the officer class produced a huge range of approaches to discipline, from the 'hard but fair' school to bullying martinets. Under these conditions, the British Army's internal system of punishment and justice was vigorously exercised.

SYSTEM OF PUNISHMENT

Most British soldiers lived under the threat of court martial and punishment. Despite the efforts of the Army Temperance Movement, for example, drunkenness was a prolific cause of infractions, including fighting between rival units, sexual assault and being drunk while on duty. Within the front lines there were myriad offences that might receive swift and harsh attention from an NCO. They could be trivial, such as a failure to perform a minor order, but could go up to crimes such as desertion, cowardice and striking an officer, for which a man could be tied to a post and shot.

Many disciplinary offences were handled immediately by NCOs, without recourse to official punishments. If matters were to be taken further, however, a soldier (corporal or below) would appear before either the company or – more seriously – the battalion commander. He might also end up, depending on rank and alleged crime, in front of one of several types of court martial, the most portentous of which was the field general court martial, which had the power to impose the death penalty.

EXTREME MEASURES

There was a variety of military punishments available to the authorities. Most common were being confined to barracks, pay deductions, loss of leave or rest periods, and various extra fatigue duties. A more extreme sentence (flogging having been abolished in the British Army in 1881), was Field Punishment No. 1. Here the convicted man was handcuffed to a fixed object, often a gun wheel, for up to 21 days, for several hours a day, through all weathers. Sometimes the man would be bound in a spreadeagled position

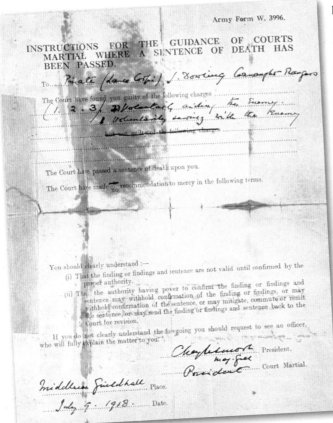

◀ This 'instruction for the guidance of courts martial' indicates a death sentence imposed on one Private (Lance Corporal) J. Dowling of the Connaught Rangers, found guilty of voluntarily aiding the enemy. The sentence was later commuted to life imprisonment.

FIRING SQUADS

A British Army firing squad consisted of 12 men. The execution would usually occur at dawn, and the selected riflemen would draw up anxiously with loaded rifles before a wooden execution post, with a subaltern and a medical officer presiding. Typically the condemned man would have been plied with drink throughout the night, so he was often carried insensible and strapped to the post, a flannelette marker pinned over his heart by the medical officer. The subaltern would then give the command to aim and fire, after which he would fire a *coup de grâce* from his revolver

into the victim's chest. The trauma of being on a firing squad meant that not all executions went smoothly, shots being delivered erratically and inaccurately. The outcome was always the same, however.

◀ *Firing squads were an unpalatable fact of life in the British Army during the First World War. Here a group of soldiers level their SMLE rifles at a German spy in Flanders, while their sergeant keeps watch from the rear.*

onto the wheel, and so could be turned and left at nauseating angles. Field Punishment No. 1 was inflicted 60,210 times in the First World War; it was harrowing both to endure and to watch, and many officers and men felt the measure was barbaric.

The ultimate punishment was, of course, the death sentence. A total of 3,080 death sentences were handed out, but by virtue of the sentence having to be confirmed by a superior authority, only 346 men were actually shot; the remainder had their sentences commuted to terms of imprisonment. Desertion constituted the bulk of capital offences, and it condemned a good number of men who we now know were suffering from shell shock. Death penalties could breed much hostility amongst companies, not least because – in a final indignity – the firing squads were composed of members of the victim's unit.

➤ *A memorial plaque sits behind an execution post in Poperinge, Belgium, a town close to the front line. Many of the men tied to the post and shot were classified as deserters. The last execution carried out here is dated 19 May 1919, six months after the end of the war.*

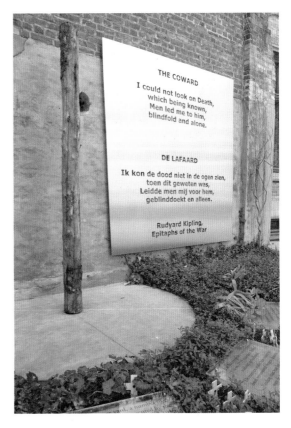

THE COWARD

I could not look on Death,
which being known,
Men led me to him,
blindfold and alone.

DE LAFAARD

Ik kon de dood niet in de ogen zien,
toen dit geweten was,
Leidde men mij voor hem,
geblinddoekt en alleen.

Rudyard Kipling,
Epitaphs of the War

THE EXPERIENCE OF BATTLE

Major battles happened on a relatively infrequent basis during the First World War, and a soldier's involvement in a major offensive was quite rare; many thousands of soldiers never participated directly in a great engagement. Yet between offensives, combat rumbled on at various levels, from minor exchanges of artillery fire through to the violent experience of trench raids.

TRENCH RAIDS

Trench raids were a common form of offensive action, typically launched to take prisoners or destroy a German position or weapon. They were usually conducted by volunteers, and they could vary dramatically in size, from an officer and a handful of men creeping stealthily across no-man's-land at night, to an entire company or battalion making a daylight assault with artillery support.

The raids were brutal affairs. Crossing no-man's-land exposed the soldiers to enemy fire, and if they made it into the opposing trenches brutal hand-to-hand combat awaited. Following the outward assault, the raiding party then had to

return across no-man's-land under the guns of a fully alert enemy, plus they faced the additional risk of being shot by nervous soldiers on their own side.

'OVER THE TOP'

For the millions of soldiers who did participate in and survive a major attack, the experience was harrowing and unforgettable. The opposing trench lines were usually blasted in advance by preparatory artillery fire, and courtesy of German counter-fire the infantry could take casualties even as they moved up to the front line.

When the hour of attack came, an officer would signal for the men to leave the trenches and advance. The speed of attack was affected by multiple factors – the need to keep unit integrity across difficult terrain; the weight of pack carried (large backpacks were generally left behind, but overall weight of kit could still exceed 60lb/27kg); over-confidence in artillery preparation; and the nature of the terrain (at Third Ypres the battlefield was so waterlogged that dozens of men drowned in mud-filled shell holes). Often such factors,

▲ *Even those who experienced the horror of war found time for humour. In this whimsical cartoon from a soldier's autograph book, Tommies peer over the hill and watch a pig sniffing around a live shell; the punchline reads 'Pork later'.*

▶ The Lewis light machine gun provided infantry units with more portable automatic fire compared to the heavy Vickers. Here a Lewis is adapted as an anti-aircraft weapon.

◀ Exhaustion etched on their faces, British stretcher-bearers attempt to carry a wounded man through knee-deep mud on the Passchendaele battlefield in 1917.

▶ The living attend to the dead in an apocalyptic scene, as the sun rises over Passchendaele in October 1917. The terrible mud also meant that many of the dead were swallowed by the battlefield where they fell.

ADVANCING TO DEATH

Private Ernest Deighton, of the King's Own Yorkshire Light Infantry, remembers the fighting on the Somme, 1916:

I were in the first row and the first one I saw were my chum, Clem Cunnington. I don't think we'd gone 20 yards when he got it straight through the chest. Machine-gun bullets. He went down, I went down. We got it in the same burst. I got it through the shoulder. I hardly noticed it at the time. I were so wild when I saw that Clem were finished.

I got up and picked up my rifle and got through the wire into their trench and straight in front there was this dugout – full of jerries, and one big fellow was on the steps facing me. I had the Mills bomb. Couldn't use my arm. I pulled the pin with my teeth and flung it down ... It was hand to hand! I went round one traverse and there was one – face-to-face. I couldn't fire one-handed, but I could use the bayonet. It was him or me – and I went first! Jab! Just like that.

and not the unrealistic dictates of commanders, reduced the pace of attack to little more than a spirited walk, although in the light of experience many offensives were conducted at a more respectable sprint.

Naturally, the most dangerous point of the attack was the advance through no-man's-land. Private Roy Bealing, Wiltshire Regiment, remembered the experience: 'When the whistle went, I threw my rifle on top of the trench and clambered out of it, grabbed the rifle and started going forward. There were shell-holes everywhere. I must have fallen half-a-dozen times before I got to the first line, and there were lads falling all over the place.'

Surviving the next hours, and subsequent days, was a trial of mind, body and luck. Soldiers' uniforms became heavy with caked mud; stomachs grumbled from lack of food; the wounded had to be evacuated and carried back to the aid stations. It was an experience of hell, and one that more than 900,000 British and Empire soldiers did not survive.

CASUALTIES OF WAR

The 4 July 1916 war diary entry for the 1st Battalion, 1st East Yorkshire Regiment, after just four days of fighting on the Somme, listed a total of 19 officers and 441 men dead and wounded. Their experience was typical. British offensives tended to make grindingly slow progress – if at all – with heavy casualties. At Passchendaele, the British sustained about 34 dead and wounded for every yard of ground taken. Yet even during the 'quiet' periods, men were regularly killed and wounded by exchanges of fire, or from the inevitable accidents while handling heavy equipment and weaponry.

THE DEAD

The British front-line Tommy became terribly familiar with death. Often the soldiers lived directly in the presence of corpses of both friends and enemies. Corporal Joe Hayles, who fought at the Somme in 1916, remembered: 'There was a terrible smell. It was so awful it nearly poisoned you. A smell of rotten flesh. The old German front line was covered with bodies – they were seven and eight deep and they had all gone black. These people had been lying since the First of July. Wicked it was! Bodies all over the place. I'll never forget it.'

Many thousands of bodies simply rotted where they fell, while others were transported to the rear, wrapped in fabric shrouds or blankets, to be buried in civilian cemeteries or mass military graves. During periods of heavy fatalities, bodies might simply be laid side by side in mass graves, awaiting more peaceful times for proper remembrance. For many of the dead this act did not come for many years: in 2008 the remains of an estimated 400 British and Australian troops were found in Fromelles, France, buried there by the Germans in July 1916.

▲ Mustard gas attacked the eyes, skin and respiratory system. Here a group of gas-blinded soldiers, injured during a German attack in 1918, form a column, led by a sighted soldier at the front.

▼ The cost of war. Three of the four brothers pictured here did not survive the war. Corporal Archie Barker (right) was the only one of the group to make it through.

▲ *Australian casualties fill up an underground advanced dressing station during the battle of Menin Road Ridge, France, 1917. The insanitary conditions of such aid stations meant that secondary infections were a serious problem for the wounded.*

THE WOUNDED

The millions of British Army soldiers wounded in the First World War were treated by the orderlies, stretcher-bearers and doctors of the Royal Army Medical Corps (RAMC). On foreign soil, a wounded soldier was treated via a chain of medical establishments. Closest to the front line was the regimental aid post (RAP), to which he was carried by battalion stretcher-bearers, after which came (in increasing distance from the front) the advanced dressing station (ADS), main dressing station (MDS), casualty clearing station (CCS) and, finally, the general and stationary hospitals. If the soldier's wounds were severe enough, then his journey would continue to hospitals back in Britain, and such injuries became known as 'Blighty wounds' (Blighty being the Hindustani term for 'Home District').

The RAMC grew to nearly 150,000 personnel by 1918 (Regular and Territorial), and it was faced with demands on medical expertise rarely experienced in history. As well as wounds from bullet and shell, it had to cope with thousands of gassed soldiers – blinded, burnt, asphyxiated or poisoned by gases such as chlorine, phosphorous and mustard. It also had to adjust to the psychological effects of industrial warfare, in the form of 80,000 'shell shock' victims. The understanding of this condition was emergent, and patients suffering from traumatic mental breakdown were often treated disdainfully or cruelly, as if they were 'malingerers'. Yet what we now call post-traumatic stress disorder (PTSD) would dog millions of soldiers in later life, not just those hospitalized for the condition.

'DULCE ET DECORUM EST'

Bent double, like old beggars under sacks,
Knock-kneed, coughing like hags, we cursed
    through sludge,
Till on the haunting flares we turned our backs
And towards our distant rest began to trudge.
Men marched asleep. Many had lost their boots
But limped on, blood-shod. All went lame; all blind;
Drunk with fatigue; deaf even to the hoots
Of gas-shells shells that dropped behind.

GAS! GAS! Quick, boys! – An ecstasy of fumbling,
Fitting the clumsy helmets just in time;
But someone still was yelling out and stumbling
And floundering like a man in fire or lime. –
Dim, through the misty panes and thick green light
As under a green sea, I saw him drowning.

In all my dreams, before my helpless sight,
He plunges at me, guttering, choking, drowning.

If in some smothering dreams you too could pace
Behind the wagon that we flung him in,
And watch the white eyes writhing in his face,
His hanging face, like a devil's sick of sin;
If you could hear, at every jolt, the blood
Come gargling from the froth-corrupted lungs,
Obscene as cancer, bitter as the cud
Of vile, incurable sores on innocent tongues, –
My friend, you would not tell with such high zest
To children ardent for some desperate glory,
The old Lie: *Dulce et decorum est*
Pro patria mori.

WILFRED OWEN, WAR POET AND BRITISH OFFICER,
KILLED IN ACTION 4 NOVEMBER 1918

COMRADES IN WAR AND PEACE

The British Army was a true cross-section of British society, containing every shade and hue of social class, occupation, community and personality type. The initial surge of volunteerism in 1914 and 1915 created battalions of men who would have previously kept very separate lives. When the Accrington Pals formed up, an onlooker noted the social composition of the recruits: 'Miners, mill-hands, office-boys, black-coats, bosses, school-boys and masters ... Young men who should have been tied to their mother's apron string ... Men of mature age, patriotic or sensing adventure or to escape from monotony.' The war took such men and bound them together in an unbelievable shared experience.

BROTHERS IN ARMS

Social mobility and the opportunities for travel were extremely limited in early 20th-century Britain, so the war at least gave unparalleled circumstance for adventure. Indeed, for many the war gave them their first and only taste of foreign travel, albeit to a war front.

▲ *Soldiers at the front lived intimately side by side, performing every human function in each other's presence. Here soldiers are washing themselves in a shell hole in France, June 1917.*

Men who lived and fought together often testified to bonds that surpassed those of family and marriage, bonds that could only be broken, at least physically, by death itself. Officer E.A. Macintosh, killed at Cambrai in 1917, had earlier written a poem about the death of one of his men, Private David Sutherland, imaginatively addressing David's father: 'You were only David's father,/ But I had fifty sons/ When we went up in the evening/ Under the arch of the guns.' Such sentiments ran both ways, with companies showing unquestionable and sometimes suicidal loyalty to junior officers.

Amongst the infantrymen themselves, the bonds were just as tight. Lieutenant Charles Carrington

▶ *Tens of thousands of soldiers suffered amputated limbs during the First World War. This soldier, one of the lucky ones, has received a set of prosthetic limbs from the Queen Mary's Convalescent Auxiliary Hospital in Roehampton, south-west London.*

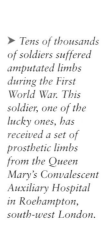

Forever comrades. A soldier with both legs amputated attends a concert for wounded veterans at the Savoy Hotel, London, in March 1916.

observed that 'A Corporal and six men in a trench were like shipwrecked sailors on a raft, completely committed to their social grouping ... everyone's life depended on the reliability of each.' Devotion to each other, as much as sense of duty or intrinsic bravery, doubtless contributed to the 500 Victoria Crosses and the 170,000 other decorations (not including bars) awarded to soldiers on the Western Front.

▶ The demobilization document for Private M.E. Brewer, listing the monies due to him on leaving the army on 27 December 1919. For many soldiers, peacetime brought a return to financial hardship in a world replete with unemployed veterans.

A NEW LIFE

Military Medal winner George Coppard remembered the reality of life back in Britain:

I joined the queue for jobs as messengers, window cleaners and scullions. It was a complete let down for thousands of men like me, and for some young officers too. It was a common sight in London to see ex-officers with barrel organs, refusing to earn a living as beggars. Single men picked up twenty-one shillings a week unemployment pay as a special allowance, but there were no jobs for the 'heroes' who had won the war.

HOMECOMING

In November 1918, the guns fell silent on the Western Front, and millions of men were demobilized, returning home to old lives. The process took time, with demobilization continuing until 1922, although the bulk of soldiers were sent home within a year of the Armistice. Officers and men alike testified to the difficulty of fitting back into civilian life. The job market was flooded by those seeking employment opportunities, and being a combat veteran carried little weight when so many others shared the status (see panel). All the army provided was a cheap demobilization suit (soldiers were allowed to keep various items of uniform, particularly the greatcoat) or a clothing allowance, limited unemployment benefit and a 'Certificate of Employment', explaining something of the soldier's skills gained in the army. Often the jobs were found by soldiers who had served least time in the army – they had only a short break from the skills of employment, whereas for 'old timers' civilian work was a distant memory.

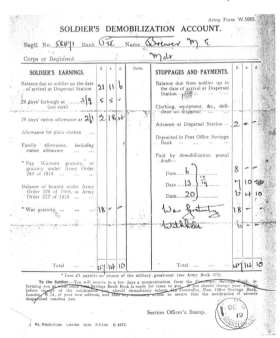

FURTHER AFIELD

Although the Western Front was by far the largest deployment of British troops in the First World War, we should not forget that tens of thousands of Tommies served in more far-flung corners of the globe. British deployments included China, East Africa, Mesopotamia, Sinai, Palestine, the Balkans and the North-West Frontier. Some of these deployments were marginal, involving just a few thousand men, while others were major and costly campaigns – the Gallipoli campaign from April 1915 to January 1916 was an outright disaster.

▲ Hot and weary, men of the Royal Fusiliers return from the trenches through Gully Ravine at Gallipoli, Turkey, in 1915. The battle of Gully Ravine took place 28 June–5 July that year, and was largely successful despite a high number of casualties.

FIGHTING THE CLIMATE

Climate and environment posed some of the greatest challenges for British soldiers serving outside European battlefields. Middle Eastern and African postings were particularly arduous, the soldiers having to cope with equatorial temperatures, tropical diseases and dangerous wildlife, as well as the enemy. Disease was a particularly pressing issue. In the East African campaign, cholera, malaria, typhoid, dysentery and other afflictions caused 30 British casualties for every man killed in combat. Even closer to home, in the Dardanelles, disease also made daily life a misery, as testified by Sergeant W. H. Lench at Gallipoli in 1915: 'The water was death; the bully beef was death; everything was death. I was afraid to eat a thing. It terrified me; it made me feel dead. A man would pass me holding his stomach, groaning in agony, and a few minutes later I would take him off the latrine, dead. The men contracted dysentery and fever every day. The bullets did not take a big toll. It was the death of germs.'

▶ Britain relied heavily on its Commonwealth troops to fight in the First World War. This photograph shows New Zealanders fitting ammunition into machine-gun belts.

▲ *A rather romantic photograph of British Army soldiers in Egypt, c. 1916. As well as fighting for Europe, the British Army also had to fight abroad to preserve an existing empire.*

▲ *Early morning, 9 December 1917: the Mayor of Jerusalem (centre, with walking stick) attempts to deliver a letter surrendering the city to Sergeants James Sedgwick and Frederick Hurcomb (fourth and seventh from left) of the 2/19th Battalion, London Regiment. The white flag seen here (a sheet from a hospital bed, nailed to a broomstick) is now in the Imperial War Museum, London.*

The environment threw up other threats. In Sinai and Palestine, sandstorms would fill the air with choking sand particles (see panel). Snake bites were a regular threat on East African patrols. The hot-climate deployments also brought the ever-present burden of blazing sunshine. In Syria and Palestine, British and Commonwealth forces required 400,000 gallons (1.5 million litres) of water every day just to keep men and mounts hydrated. Although Tommies were issued with a light khaki drill tropical uniform, and a lightweight cork pith helmet, the effort required to operate was considerable. Private Robert Harding, 1/4th Battalion Dorset Regiment, described a march in the Middle East: 'We trudge on, and men bow beneath the weight of ammunition, equipment, and rifle. The brazen sun burns; clothes become wet with sweat; topees [lightweight sun hats] heavy and big. At hourly halts we sink to the ground, and rise again with stiff joints and aching shoulders. At given times we drink and march again, until the sun sinks low and tinges the desert red.'

FORGOTTEN CORNERS

The British and Commonwealth campaign in Gallipoli brought horrors every bit as grim as those experienced on the Western Front, plus more than 200,000 Allied casualties. Yet even the smaller campaigns were costly. The East African theatre produced around 10,000 British dead, 70 per cent from disease. Those who survived, however, experienced cultures well beyond the familiarity of Europe, and brought back some evocative and emotional memories.

SAPPER BONSER REMEMBERS

'September of this year found us on the borders of Palestine. The chief hardship was lack of water – a good wash was a luxury. Our final preparations for the advance (1917) took place in a sandstorm. For three days we were working with goggles over our eyes and handkerchiefs round mouth and nostrils. The job was recovering and loading cable ready for the dash up. It was impossible to see a man 20 yards away; there was sand all over our perspiring bodies, sand on every mouthful of food we ate, and a sip of tepid water left sand on our lips. Half the fellows were suffering from dysentery pains and passing blood.'

SAPPER H.P. BONSER, ROYAL ENGINEERS (SIGNALS)

GRAVES AND MONUMENTS

Wherever you are in Britain, you are rarely any great distance from one of the *c*. 45,000 memorials to the dead of the First World War. As few bodies were repatriated (the decision was made to bury them where fallen), bereaved families and communities created some focus for their loss through memorials listing the names of the dead. They range from little more than a plaque fixed to the outside of a factory or town hall, through to major monumental sculpture.

The extent of the lists can be sobering, given the size of the communities. For example, the small rural village of Kirby-le-Soken in Essex lists no fewer than 34 war dead, despite the fact that the total village population probably numbered around only 1,000 at the time. Other memorials list hundreds of names, common surnames often indicating multiple losses within individual families. The Tomb of the Unknown Warrior in Westminster Abbey in London, by contrast, holds the remains of just one unidentified serviceman, but in so doing represents the tens of thousands who died in anonymity.

It is in the numerous cemeteries and memorials of France and Belgium that we gain a true sense of the huge loss of the First World War. The Thiepval Memorial to the missing alone bears the names of 73,357 Allied soldiers who died in the Somme area in 1916–18 but found no permanent grave, while the Étaples Military Cemetery contains no less than 10,733 British and Commonwealth graves from 1914–18. Such memorials remind us that many British Tommies paid the ultimate price for their service, a long way from home.

▲ *The Tomb of the Unknown Warrior, whose remains were brought from France and buried in the nave of Westminster Abbey on 11 November 1920.*

◄ *The sobering legacy of the First World War. Flatiron Copse Cemetery is just one of numerous British sites of remembrance around France and Belgium, and contains the remains of more than 1,100 identified British soldiers.*